CALIFORNIAN COOKING

GALLERY BOOKS
An Imprint of W. H. Smith Publishers Inc.
112 Madison Avenue
New York City 10016

INTRODUCTION

As varied as its landscapes, as vibrant as its climate, California's food is innovative, but with an eye to its heritage. Nothing if not cosmopolitan, California cuisine draws heavily on the dishes of China, Mexico and Italy, from where many of the state's first citizens came. Contemporary chefs have studied French cuisine, experimented and come up with spirited versions of classics that reflect today's style of eating. California's climate and location have had a benevolent influence on its cuisine from the start. Fruits and vegetables flourish, vineyards produce grapes for wines that rival those of France, and miles of scenic coastline provide an exciting selection of seafood. All this beautifully fresh food has made the trend to healthier eating possible and very palatable.

The fresher the food, the better it stands on its own. That is why contemporary California cooks favor light sauces on simply cooked fish, poultry and meat, and light dressings for salads that let the flavors of the individual ingredients shine through. Above all, food from California is fun to eat.

Trends set here usually spread throughout the country. Given the enthusiasm and adventurous spirit of California cooks, we will have yet more to look forward to.

SERVES 6-8

CIOPPINO

California's famous and delicious fish
stew is Italian in heritage; but a close
relative of French Bouillabaisse, too.

1lb spinach, well washed
1 tbsp each chopped fresh basil, thyme, rosemary and
  sage
2 tbsps chopped fresh marjoram
4 tbsps chopped parsley
1 large red pepper, seeded and finely chopped
2 cloves garlic, crushed
24 large fresh clams or 48 mussels, well scrubbed
1 large crab, cracked
1lb monkfish or rock salmon (huss)
12 large shrimp, cooked and unpeeled
1lb canned plum tomatoes and juice
2 tbsps tomato paste
4 tbsps olive oil
Pinch salt and pepper
½-1 cup dry white wine
Water

1. Chop the spinach leaves roughly after removing any tough stems.

2. Combine the spinach with the herbs, chopped red pepper and garlic, and set aside.

3. Discard any clams or mussels with broken shells or ones that do not close when tapped. Place the shellfish in the bottom of a large pot and sprinkle over a layer of the spinach mixture.

4. Prepare the crab as for Crab Louis, leaving the shells on the claws after cracking them slightly. Place the crab on top of the spinach and then add another spinach layer.

5. Add the fish and a spinach layer, followed by the shrimp and any remaining spinach.

6. Mix the tomatoes, tomato paste, oil, wine and seasonings and pour over the seafood and spinach.

7. Cover the pot and simmer the mixture for about 40 minutes. If more liquid is necessary, add water. Spoon into soup bowls, dividing the fish and shell fish evenly.

Step 3 Place well scrubbed clams or mussels in the bottom of a large pot, sprinkling over spinach mixture.

Step 6 Pour the tomato paste and wine mixture over the layered seafood and spinach

Cook's Notes

Time
Preparation takes abut 40 minutes and cooking takes about 40 minutes.

Preparation
Soup must be eaten immediately after cooking. It does not keep or reheat well.

Variation
The choice of seafood or fish may be changed to suit your own taste and budget. For special occasions, add lobster.

SERVES 4

Avocado Soup

Avocados feature frequently in
California cooking. A cold soup
like this makes an easy summer meal.

2 large ripe avocados
1½ cups natural yogurt
2 cups chicken or vegetable stock
½ clove garlic, minced
Juice of 1 lemon
2 tsps chopped fresh oregano
Salt and white pepper
Chopped parsley to garnish

Step 1 Tap the stone with a knife and twist to remove it.

Step 1 Cut the avocados in half and twist to separate.

Step 2 Place the avocado cut side down on a worktop, score the skin and pull it backwards to remove.

1. Cut the avocados in half lengthwise and twist to separate. Tap the stone sharply with a knife and twist to remove.

2. Place the avocado halves cut side down on a flat surface. Score the skin with a sharp knife and then peel the strips of skin backwards to remove them.

3. Cut the avocado into pieces and place in a food processor. Reserve 4 tbsps yogurt and add the remaining yogurt and other ingredients, except the parsley, to the avocado. Process until smooth and chill thoroughly.

4. Pour the soup into bowls or a tureen and garnish with reserved yogurt. Sprinkle with parsley and serve chilled.

Cook's Notes

Time
Preparation takes about 20-25 minutes. The soup should chill for about 2 hours in the refrigerator before serving.

Cook's Tip
The lemon juice, plus the slight acidity of the yogurt, will keep the avocado from turning brown. However, serve the soup on the same day it is prepared.

Preparation
Check the avocado skins and be sure to scrape off any flesh that remains attached to them before processing the ingredients.

CALIFORNIAN SHRIMP AND SCALLOP STIR-FRY

Stir-frying came to California with Chinese settlers who worked
on the railroads. It's the perfect way to cook seafood.

3 tbsps oil
4 tbsps pine nuts
1lb uncooked shrimp
1lb shelled scallops, quartered if large
2 tsps grated fresh ginger
1 small red or green chili, seeded and finely chopped
2 cloves garlic, finely chopped
1 large red pepper, seeded and cut into 1″ diagonal
  pieces
8oz fresh spinach, stalks removed and leaves well
  washed and shredded
4 green onions, cut in ½″ diagonal pieces
4 tbsps fish or chicken stock
4 tbsps light soy sauce
4 tbsps rice wine or dry sherry
1 tbsp cornstarch

1. Heat oil in a wok and add the pine nuts. Cook over low
heat, stirring continuously until lightly browned. Remove
with a draining spoon and drain on paper towels.

2. Add the shrimp and scallops to the oil remaining in the
wok and stir over moderate heat until shellfish is beginning
to look opaque and firm and the shrimp look pink.

3. Add the ginger, chili, garlic and red pepper and cook a
few minutes over moderately high heat.

4. Add the spinach and onion, and stir-fry briefly. Mix the
remaining ingredients together and pour over the ingredients in the wok.

5. Turn up the heat to bring the liquid quickly to the boil,
stirring ingredients constantly. Once the liquid thickens and
clears, stir in the pine nuts and serve immediately.

Step 1 Cook pine
nuts in oil until
they are light
brown.

Step 2 Cook
shellfish until
shrimp begin to
turn pink and
scallops lose their
transparency.

Step 5 When all
ingredients are
added, cook
briskly to thicken
the sauce.

Cook's Notes

Time
Preparation takes about 35
minutes, cooking takes about
8-10 minutes.

Preparation
Because cooking time is so
short, be sure to prepare all
ingredients and have them ready
before beginning to stir-fry.

Economy
Eliminate scallops and cut the
quantity of shrimp in half.
Make up the difference with a firm
whitefish cut into 1″ pieces.

SERVES 4-6

CAESAR SALAD

Both Los Angeles and Tijuana take credit
for this salad, said to have been concocted one
evening from the only ingredients left in the kitchen.

6 anchovy fillets, soaked in 4 tbsps milk
1 cup olive oil
1 clove garlic, left whole
4 slices French bread, cut into ½″ cubes
1 egg, cooked 1 minute
1 head Romaine lettuce
Juice of 1 small lemon
Salt and pepper
4 tbsps grated Parmesan cheese

paper towels.

3. Break the cooked egg into a bowl and beat well with the lemon juice, salt and pepper. Toss the lettuce with the remaining garlic oil and anchovies. Add the egg mixture and toss to coat well. Place in a clean serving bowl and sprinkle over the croûtons and Parmesan cheese. Serve at room temperature.

Step 2 Fry the cubes of French bread in the hot oil, stirring them constantly for even browning.

Step 3 To make the dressing, break the egg into the bowl and mix well with the lemon juice and seasoning until slightly thickened.

Step 3 Add the oil to the lettuce separately and then toss with the egg dressing mixture.

1. Leave the anchovies to soak in the milk for 15 minutes. Rinse and pat dry on paper towels. Chop roughly.

2. Crush the garlic and leave in the oil for about 30 minutes. Heat all but 6 tbsps of the oil in a frying pan until hot. Fry the cubes of bread until golden brown, stirring constantly with a metal spoon for even browning. Drain on

Cook's Notes

Time
Preparation takes about 30 minutes and cooking takes about 3-5 minutes for the croûtons.

Cook's Tip
Soaking anchovy fillets in milk before using them neutralizes the strong salty taste.

Watchpoint
Remove the croûtons from the hot fat when just barely brown enough. They continue to cook slightly in their own heat as they drain.

SERVES 4

GREEN GODDESS SALAD

Californians' love of salads and
avocados combine in this fresh
recipe named for its green dressing.

8 anchovy fillets, soaked in milk, rinsed and dried
1 green onion, chopped
2 tbsps chopped fresh tarragon
3 tbsps chopped chives
4 tbsps chopped parsley
1 cup prepared mayonnaise
½ cup natural yogurt
2 tbsps tarragon vinegar
Pinch sugar and cayenne pepper
1 large head lettuce
1lb cooked chicken or seafood
1 avocado, peeled and sliced or cubed
1 tbsp lemon juice

1. Combine all the ingredients, except the lettuce, avocado and chicken or shellfish in a food processor. Work the ingredients until smooth, well mixed and green. Leave in the refrigerator at least 1 hour for the flavors to blend.

2. Shred the lettuce or tear into bite-size pieces and arrange on plates.

3. Top the lettuce with the cooked chicken cut into strips or cubes. If using crab or lobster, cut the meat into bite-size pieces. Shelled shrimp or mussels can be left whole.

4. Spoon the dressing over the chicken or seafood. Brush the avocado slices or toss the cubes with lemon juice and garnish the salad. Serve any remaining dressing separately.

Step 1 The dressing should be very well blended and light green after working in a food processor. Alternatively, use a hand blender.

Step 3 Arrange lettuce on individual plates and top with shredded chicken or shellfish.

Cook's Notes

Time
Preparation takes about 30 minutes.

Preparation
Dressing may be prepared ahead of time and kept in the refrigerator for a day or two.

Serving Ideas
The dressing may be served as a dip for vegetable crudités or with a tossed salad.

SERVES 4-6

CHINA BEACH SALAD

Named for a stretch of beach near San Francisco,
this recipe reflects the Chinese heritage in California's
past and its present passion for salads.

1lb cooked, peeled shrimp
1lb seedless white grapes, halved if large
6 sticks celery, thinly sliced on diagonal
4oz toasted flaked almonds
4oz canned water chestnuts, sliced or diced
8oz canned lichees or 12oz fresh litchis, peeled
1 small fresh pineapple, peeled, cored and cut into
    pieces
1½ cups mayonnaise
1 tbsp honey
1 tbsp light soy sauce
2 tbps mild curry powder
Juice of half a lime
Chinese cabbage or Belgian endive (chicory)

1. Combine the shrimp, grapes, celery, almonds, water chestnuts and litchis in a large bowl. Trim off the top and bottom of the pineapple and quarter. Slice off the points of each quarter to remove the core.

2. Slice the pineapple skin away and cut the flesh into bite-size pieces. Add to the shrimp and toss to mix.

3. Break the Chinese cabbage or endive and wash them well. If using Chinese cabbage, shred the leafy part finely, saving the thicker ends of the leaves for other use. Place the Chinese cabbage on salad plates. Mix the remaining dressing ingredients thoroughly. Pile the salad ingredients onto the leaves and spoon over some of the dressing, leaving the ingredients showing. Separate chicory leaves and arrange them whole. Serve remaining dressing separately.

Step 1 Trim the point of each quarter of pineapple to remove the core.

Step 2 Use a serrated fruit knife to slice between the skin and pineapple flesh.

Step 2 Add pineapple pieces to the shrimp and mix well.

 *Cook's Notes*

 Time
Preparation takes about 30 minutes.

 Serving Ideas
Serve as a main course salad for lunch or a light dinner. Serve in smaller quantities as an appetizer.

 Variation
Other seafood may be substituted for the shrimp. Use crab, lobster or shellfish such as mussels.

SERVES 6

WALNUT GROVE SALAD

Walnut Grove is a town famous for its walnuts! They add their crunch to a colorful variation on coleslaw.

1 small head red cabbage
1 avocado, peeled and cubed
1 carrot, grated
4 green onions, shredded
1 cup chopped walnuts
6 tbsps oil
2 tbsps white wine vinegar
2 tsps dry mustard
Salt and pepper

Step 1 Remove the core from the cabbage quarters and shred with a sharp knife or use a food processor.

1. Cut the cabbage in quarters and remove the core. Use a large knife to shred finely or use the thick slicing blade on a food processor.

2. Prepare the avocado as for Avocado Soup and cut it into small cubes.

3. Combine the cabbage, avocado and shredded carrot with the onions and walnuts in a large bowl.

4. Mix the remaining ingredients together well and pour over the salad. Toss carefully to avoid breaking up the avocado. Chill before serving.

Step 4 Mixing the salad with your hands prevents the avocado from breaking up too much.

Cook's Notes

Time
Preparation takes about 25-30 minutes.

Serving Ideas
Serve as a side dish with chicken or as part of a salad buffet.

Preparation
The salad may be prepared a day in advance and the avocado and dressing added just before serving.

SERVES 4

CRAB LOUIS

This salad is legendary on Fisherman's
Wharf in San Francisco. Once tasted,
it is sure to become a favorite.

2 large cooked crabs
1 head iceberg lettuce
4 large tomatoes
4 hard-boiled eggs
16 black olives
1 cup prepared mayonnaise
4 tbsps whipping cream
4 tbsps chili sauce or tomato chutney
½ green pepper, seeded and finely diced
3 green onions, finely chopped
Salt and pepper

Step 1 Turn crabs over and press up with thumbs to separate the under-body from the shell.

1. To prepare the crabs, break off the claws and set them aside. Turn the crabs over and press up with thumbs to separate the body from the shell of each.

2. Cut the body into quarters and use a skewer to pick out the white meat. Discard the stomach sac and the lungs (dead-man's fingers). Scrape out the brown meat from the shell to use, if desired.

3. Crack the large claws and legs and remove the meat. Break into shreds, discarding any shell or cartilage. Combine all the meat and set it aside.

4. Shred the lettuce finely, quarter the tomatoes and chop the eggs.

5. Combine the mayonnaise, cream, chilli sauce or chutney, green pepper and spring onions and mix well.

6. Arrange the shredded lettuce on serving plates and divide the crab meat evenly.

7. Spoon some of the dressing over each serving of crab and sprinkle with the chopped egg. Garnish each serving with tomato wedges and olives and serve the remaining dressings separately.

Cook's Notes

Time
Preparation takes about 30-40 minutes.

Preparation
To shred lettuce finely, break off the leaves and stack them up a few at a time. Use a large, sharp knife to cut across the leaves into thin shreds.

Variation
Frozen crab meat may be used instead of fresh. Make sure it is completely defrosted and well drained before using. Pick through the meat to remove any bits of shell or cartilage left behind.

SERVES 4

TOMATO AND ORANGE SALAD WITH MOZZARELLA AND BASIL

Juicy tomatoes combine with mozzarella and basil in this
classic Italian salad given Californian flair with bright oranges.

4 large tomatoes
4 small oranges
8oz mozzarella cheese
8 fresh basil leaves
4 tbsps olive oil
1 tbsp balsamic vinegar
Salt and pepper

Step 2 Peel the oranges in thin strips to help preserve the round shape of the fruit.

1. Remove the cores from the tomatoes and slice into rounds about ¼ inch thick.

2. Cut the slice from the top and bottom of each orange and, using a serrated fruit knife, remove the peel in thin strips. Make sure to cut off all the white pith. Slices oranges into ¼ inch thick rounds. Slice the mozzarella cheese into the same thickness.

3. Arrange the tomatoes, oranges and mozzarella in overlapping circles, alternating each ingredient.

4. Use scissors to shred the basil leaves finely, and sprinkle over the salad.

5. Mix the remaining ingredients together well and spoon over the salad. Chill briefly before serving.

Step 3 Arrange the ingredients in overlapping circles.

Step 4 Use scissors to finely shred the basil leaves over the top of the salad.

Cook's Notes

Time
Preparation takes about 20-25 minutes.

Preparation
Shred the basil leaves just before serving, since they tend to turn black if cut and left to stand.

Buying Guide
Balsamic vinegar is available from delicatessens and Italian grocers. Substitute white wine vinegar if not available.

SERVES 4

SQUASH WITH CALIFORNIAN BLUEBERRIES

This vegetable dish will steal the scene at any meal,
so serve it with simply cooked poultry or meat.

2 acorn squash
1 small apple, peeled and chopped
4 tbsps light brown sugar
Freshly grated nutmeg
4 tbsps butter or margarine
6oz fresh or frozen blueberries

1. Cut the squash in half lengthwise. Scoop out the seeds and discard them.

2. Fill the hollows with the chopped apple.

3. Sprinkle on the sugar and nutmeg and dot with the butter or margarine.

4. Place the squash in a baking dish and pour in about 1″ of water. Bake, covered, for 40-45 minutes at 375°F. Uncover, add the blueberries and cook an additional 10 minutes.

Step 2 Fill the hollows with apple and sprinkle on sugar, nutmeg and butter.

Step 4 Place the squash in a baking dish and pour in enough water to measure 1 inch.

Cook's Notes

Time
Preparation takes about 30 minutes and cooking takes about 50-55 minutes.

Preparation
If using frozen blueberries, drain them well and shorten the cooking time by about 5 minutes.

Buying Guide
Acorn squash are dark green with the occasional orange patch. Choose a squash that has a very hard rind on the outside. The squash will keep uncut in a cool place for about a month or two.

SERVES 6

ZUCCHINI SLIPPERS

Italian immigrants to California made
the zucchini squash a popular food
item used in many delicious recipes.

6 even-sized zucchini
4oz cottage cheese, drained
4oz grated Colby cheese
1 small red pepper, seeded and chopped
2 tbsps chopped parsley
Pinch salt and cayenne pepper
1 large egg
Watercress or parsley to garnish

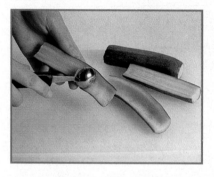

Step 2 Cut the pre-cooked zucchini in half lengthwise and scoop out the center with a teaspoon or melon baller.

1. Trim the ends of the zucchini and cook in boiling salted water for about 8 minutes, or steam for 10 minutes.

2. Remove from the water or steamer and cut in half. Allow to cool slightly and then scoop out the center, leaving a narrow margin of flesh on the skin to form a shell. Invert each zucchini slipper onto a paper towel to drain, reserving the scooped-out flesh.

3. Chop the flesh and mix with the remaining ingredients.

4. Spoon filling into the shells and arrange in a greased baking dish. Bake, uncovered, in a pre-heated 350°F oven for 15 minutes. Broil, if desired, to brown the top. Garnish with watercress or parsley.

Step 4 Use a small spoon to fill the zucchini neatly.

Step 4 Bake until the cheese melts and the filling begins to bubble slightly. Grill at this point, if desired.

Cook's Notes

Time
Preparation takes about 30 minutes and cooking takes about 23-25 minutes.

Preparation
The dish may be prepared ahead of time and kept in the refrigerator overnight to bake the next day.

Serving Ideas
Serve as a vegetable side dish with meat, poultry of fish. Alternatively, serve as an appetizer. Double the quantity and serve as a vegetarian main course.

Watchpoint
Be sure the zucchini are very well drained before filling. Baking will draw out any excess moisture and make the dish watery.

SERVES 4

VEGETABLE RIBBONS WITH PESTO

There is no substitute for fresh basil in this sauce. Prepare
it in the summer when basil is plentiful to freeze for later.

2 large zucchini, ends trimmed
2 medium carrots, peeled
1 large or 2 small leeks, trimmed, halved and well
　washed
1 cup shelled pistachio nuts
2 small shallots, chopped
2-3oz fresh basil leaves
1-1½ cups olive oil
Salt and pepper

1. Cut the zucchini and carrots into long, thin slices with a mandolin or by hand. A food processor will work but the slices will be short.

2. Cut the leeks into lengths the same size as the zucchini and carrots. Make sure the leeks are well rinsed in between all layers. Cut into long, thin strips.

3. Using a large, sharp knife, cut the zucchini and carrot slices into long, thin strips about the thickness of 2 matchsticks. The julienne blade of a food processor will produce strips that are too fine to use.

4. Place the carrot strips in a pan of boiling salted water and cook for about 3-4 minutes or until tender crisp. Drain and rinse under cold water. Cook the zucchini strips separately for about 2-3 minutes and add the leek strips

during the last 1 minute of cooking. Drain and rinse the vegetables and leave with the carrots to drain dry.

5. Place the nuts, shallots and basil in the bowl of a food processor or in a blender and chop finely.

6. Reserve about 3 tbsps of the olive oil for later use. With the machine running, pour the remaining oil through the funnel in a thin, steady stream. Use enough oil to bring the mixture to the consistency of mayonnaise. Add seasoning to taste.

7. Place reserved oil in a large pan and, when hot, add the drained vegetables. Season and toss over moderate heat until heated through. Add the pesto sauce and toss gently to coat the vegetables. Serve immediately.

Step 3 Stack several lengths of zucchini and carrot and cut into long julienne strips.

Cook's Notes

Time
Preparation takes about 30-40 minutes and cooking takes about 45 minutes.

Serving Ideas
Serve as a side dish with broiled meat, poultry or fish and prepare larger quantities for a vegetarian main course. Parmesan cheese may be sprinkled on top.

Preparation
Pesto can be prepared several days in advance and kept, covered, in the refrigerator. Pesto sauce can also be frozen for up to 6 months.

SERVES 4

NapaValley Artichokes

The Napa Valley is wine growing country, so
white wine is a natural choice for cooking
one of California's best-loved vegetables.

4 globe artichokes
4 tbsps olive oil
1 clove garlic, left whole
1 small bay leaf
1 sprig fresh rosemary
2 parsley stalks
4 black peppercorns
2 lemon slices
1 cup dry white wine
1 tbsp chopped parsley
Pinch salt and pepper
Lemon slices to garnish

1. Trim stems on the base of the artichokes so that they sit upright. Peel off any damaged bottom leaves.

2. Trim the spiny tips off all the leaves with scissors.

3. Trim the top 1″ off the artichokes with a sharp knife.

4. Place the artichokes in a large, deep pan with all the ingredients except the parsley.

5. Cover the pan and cook about 40 minutes, or until artichokes are tender and bottom leaves pull away easily. Drain upside down on paper towels.

6. Boil the cooking liquid to reduce slightly. Strain, add parsley and serve with the artichokes. Garnish with lemon slices.

Step 1 Trim the stems on the base of the artichokes so they sit level.

Step 3 Use a large, sharp knife to trim the top 1 inch of the artichokes.

Cook's Notes

 Time
Preparation takes about 30 minutes and cooking takes about 40 minutes.

Serving Ideas
Place artichokes on individual plates and spoon over the sauce or serve it separately for dipping. To eat, pull off the leaves, beginning with the bottom one, and eat the fleshy thicker part at the base of each leaf. When only the fine purple leaves in the center remain, pull them off and discard them. Using a spoon, scrape away the thistle and discard it. The base may be eaten with the dipping sauce.

SERVES 4

SAN FRANCISCO RICE

This rice and pasta dish has been popular for
a long time in San Francisco, where it was invented.

4oz uncooked long grain rice
4oz uncooked spaghetti, broken into 2″ pieces
3 tbsps oil
4 tbsps sesame seeds
2 tbsps chopped chives
Salt and pepper
1½ cups chicken, beef or vegetable stock
1 tbsp soy sauce
2 tbsps chopped parsley

1. Rinse the rice and pasta to remove starch, and leave to drain dry.

2. Heat the oil in a large frying pan and add the dried rice and pasta. Cook over moderate heat to brown the rice and pasta, stirring continuously.

3. Add the sesame seeds and cook until the rice, pasta and seeds are golden brown.

4. Add the chives, salt and pepper, and pour over 1 cup stock. Stir in the soy sauce and bring to the boil.

5. Cover and cook about 20 minutes, or until the rice and pasta are tender and the stock is absorbed. Add more of the reserved stock as necessary. Do not let the rice and pasta dry out during cooking.

6. Fluff up the grains of rice with a fork and sprinkle with the parsley before serving.

Step 2 Cook the rice and pasta in the oil until just beginning to brown.

Step 3 Add the sesame seeds and cook until the rice, pasta and seeds are golden brown.

Step 5 Cook until all the liquid is absorbed and the pasta and rice are tender.

Cook's Notes

Time
Preparation takes about 25 minutes and cooking takes about 20 minutes or more.

Preparation
If desired, once the stock is added the mixture may be cooked in a pre-heated 375°F oven. Cook for about 20 minutes, checking the level of liquid occasionally and adding more stock if necessary.

Serving Ideas
Serve as a side dish with meat or poultry. Give it an Italian flavor by omitting sesame seeds, chives and soy sauce. Substitute Parmesan and basil instead.

SERVES 4

CALIFORNIA WILD RICE PILAFF

Wild rice adds a nutty taste and a texture contrast
to rice pilaff. It's good as a side dish or stuffing.

4oz uncooked long-grain rice, rinsed
2oz wild rice, rinsed
1 tbsp oil
1 tbsp butter or margarine
2 sticks celery, finely chopped
2 green onions
4 tbsps chopped walnuts or pecans
4 tbsps raisins
1½ cups chicken or vegetable stock

Step 3 Cook both rices in butter and oil until the white rice looks clear. Stir constantly.

1. Heat the oil in a frying pan and drop in the butter.

2. When foaming, add both types of rice.

3. Cook until the white rice looks clear.

4. Add celery and chop the green onions, reserving the dark green tops to use as a garnish. Add the white part of the onions to the rice and celery and cook briefly to soften.

5. Add the walnuts or pecans, raisins and stock. Bring to the boil, cover and cook until the rice absorbs the liquid and is tender. Sprinkle with reserved chopped onion tops.

Step 5 Add remaining ingredients and, if desired, transfer to an ovenproof casserole for the remainder of cooking.

Cook's Notes

 Time
Preparation takes about 25 minutes and cooking takes about 20 minutes.

 Serving Ideas
Delicious served as a side dish for chicken or used as a stuffing for Cornish hens or other small game birds.

 Buying Guide
Wild rice is not really a rice but a grain. It is fairly expensive but it can be used in small quantities. Wild rice is available in delicatessens and specialty food shops.

 Preparation
This pilaff may also be cooked in the oven in the same manner as San Francisco Rice.

SERVES 4

SPICY ORIENTAL NOODLES

A most versatile vegetable dish, this
goes well with meat or stands alone
for a vegetarian main course.

8oz Chinese noodles (medium thickness)
5 tbsps oil
4 carrots, peeled
8oz broccoli
12 Chinese mushrooms, soaked 30 minutes
1 clove garlic, peeled
4 green onions, diagonally sliced
1-2 tsps chili sauce, mild or hot
4 tbsps soy sauce
4 tbsps rice wine or dry sherry
2 tsps cornstarch

1. Cook noodles in boiling salted water for about 4-5 minutes. Drain well, rinse under hot water to remove starch and drain again. Toss with about 1 tbsp of the oil to prevent sticking.

2. Using a large, sharp knife or Chinese cleaver, slice the carrots thinly on the diagonal.

3. Cut the flowerets off the stems of the broccoli and divide into even-sized but not too small sections. Slice the stalks thinly on the diagonal. If they seem tough, peel them before slicing.

4. Place the vegetables in boiling water for about 2 minutes to blanch. Drain and rinse under cold water to stop the cooking, and leave to drain dry.

5. Remove and discard the mushroom stems and slice the caps thinly. Set aside with the onions.

6. Heat a wok and add the remaining oil with the garlic clove. Leave the garlic in the pan while the oil heats and then remove it. Add the carrots and broccoli and stir-fry about 1 minute. Add mushrooms and onions and continue to stir-fry, tossing the vegetables in the pan continuously.

7. Combine chili sauce, soy sauce, wine and cornstarch, mixing well. Pour over the vegetables and cook until the sauce clears. Toss with the noodles and heat them through and serve immediately.

Step 7 Cook vegetables and sauce ingredients until cornstarch thickens and clears.

Cook's Notes

Time
Preparation takes about 25 minutes and cooking takes about 7-8 minutes.

Buying Guide
Chinese noodles, mushrooms and chili sauce are all available from Chinese groceries, gourmet food stores and larger supermarkets.

Serving Ideas
Use as a side dish with chicken, meat or fish, or serve as an appetizer. May also be served cold as a salad.

SERVES 4-6

FETTUCINE ESCARGOTS WITH LEEKS AND SUN-DRIED TOMATOES

These dried tomatoes keep for a long time and allow you to
add a sunny taste to dishes whatever the time of year.

6 sun-dried tomatoes or 6 fresh Italian plum tomatoes
14oz canned escargots (snails), drained
12oz fresh or dried whole-wheat fettucine (tagliatelle)
3 tbsps olive oil
2 cloves garlic, crushed
1 large or 2 small leeks, trimmed, split, well washed and
   finely sliced
6 oyster, shittake or other large mushrooms
4 tbsps chicken or vegetable stock
3 tbsps dry white wine
6 tbsps heavy cream
2 tsps chopped fresh basil
2 tsps chopped fresh parsley
Salt and pepper

Step 3 Properly
dried tomatoes
will look and feel
firm, with no
remaining liquid.

1. To "sun-dry" tomatoes in the oven, cut the tomatoes in half lengthwise.

2. Use a teaspoon or your finger to scoop out about half the seeds and juice. Press gently with your palm to flatten slightly. Sprinkle both sides with salt and place tomatoes, cut side up, on a rack over a baking pan.

3. Place in the oven on the lowest possible setting, with door ajar, if neccessary, for 24 hours, checking after 12 hours. Allow to dry until no liquid is left and the tomatoes are firm. Chop roughly.

4. Drain the escargots well and dry with paper towels.

5. Place the fettucine in boiling salted water and cook for about 10-12 minutes, or until al dente. Drain, rinse under hot water and leave in a colander to drain dry.

6. Meanwhile, heat the olive oil in a frying pan and add the garlic and leeks. Cook slowly to soften slightly. Add the mushrooms and cook until the leeks are tender crisp. Remove to a plate. Add the drained escargots to the pan and cook over high heat for about 2 minutes, stirring constantly.

7. Pour on the stock and wine and bring to the boil. Boil to reduce by about a quarter and add the cream and tomatoes. Bring to the boil then cook slowly for about 3 minutes. Add the herbs, salt and pepper to taste. Add the leeks, mushrooms and fettucine to the pan and heat through. Serve immediately.

Cook's Notes

Time
Preparation takes about 24 hours for the tomatoes to dry and about 15-20 minutes to finish the dish.

Serving Ideas
Serve as an appetizer or a main course with salad and bread. Grated Parmesan cheese may be sprinkled on top, if desired.

Variation
Escargots are not to everyone's taste, so substitute more mushrooms, cooked shrimp or spicy sausage, as desired.

SERVES 6

CHICKEN MONTEREY

There's a touch of Mexican flavor in this
chicken recipe with its accompaniment
of colorful and spicy salsa.

6 boned chicken breasts
Grated rind and juice of 1 lime
2 tbsps olive oil
Coarsely ground black pepper
6 tbsps whole grain mustard
2 tsps paprika
4 ripe tomatoes, peeled, seeded and quartered
2 shallots, chopped
1 clove garlic, crushed
½ Jalapeno pepper or other chili, seeded and chopped
1 tsp wine vinegar
Pinch salt
2 tbsps chopped fresh cilantro (coriander)
Whole coriander leaves to garnish

Step 1 Marinate chicken in a shallow dish, turning occasionally to coat.

1. Place chicken breasts in a shallow dish with the lime rind and juice, oil, pepper, mustard and paprika. Marinate for about 1 hour, turning occasionally.

2. To peel tomatoes easily, drop them into boiling water for about 5 seconds or less depending on ripeness. Place immediately in cold water. Peels should come off easily.

Step 2 Tomatoes peel easily when placed first in boiling water and then in cold.

3. Place tomatoes, shallots, garlic, chili pepper, vinegar and salt in a food processor or blender and process until coarsely chopped. Stir in the cilantro by hand.

4. Place chicken on a broiler pan and reserve the marinade. Cook chicken skin side uppermost for about 7-10 minutes, depending on how close the chicken is to the heat source. Baste frequently with the remaining marinade. Broil other side in the same way. Sprinkle with salt after broiling.

Step 4 Broil skin side of chicken until brown and crisp before turning pieces over.

5. Place chicken on serving plates and garnish top with cilantro (coriander) leaves or sprigs. Serve with a spoonful of the tomato salsa on one side.

Cook's Notes

Time
Preparation takes about 1 hour and cooking takes 14-20 minutes.

Preparation
Salsa can be prepared in advance and kept in the refrigerator. It can also be served with other poultry, meat or seafood. It also makes a good dip for vegetable crudités or tortilla chips.

Watchpoint
When preparing chili peppers, wear rubber gloves or at least be sure to wash hands thoroughly after handling them. Do not touch eyes or face before washing hands.

SERVES 6

CHICKEN JUBILEE

California cooks are creative trendsetters.
Trust them to change a cherry dessert
into a savory recipe for chicken.

6 chicken breasts, skinned and boned
Oil
1 sprig fresh rosemary
Grated rind and juice of half a lemon
1 cup dry red wine
Salt and pepper
1lb canned or fresh black cherries, pitted
2 tsps cornstarch
6 tbsps brandy

Step 1 Cook the chicken breasts until just lightly browned. Watch carefully, as skinned chicken will dry out easily.

1. Heat about 4 tbsps oil in a sauté pan over moderate heat. Place in the chicken breasts, skinned side down first. Cook until just lightly browned. Turn over and cook the second side about 2 minutes.

2. Remove any oil remaining in the pan and add the rosemary, lemon rind, wine and salt and pepper. Bring to the boil and then lower the heat.

3. Add the cherries, draining well if canned. Cook, covered, 15 minutes or until the chicken is tender. Remove the chicken and cherries and keep them warm. Discard rosemary.

4. Mix the cornstarch, lemon juice and some of the liquid from the cherries, if canned. Add several spoonfuls of the hot sauce to the cornstarch mixture. Return the mixture to the sauté pan and bring to the boil, stirring constantly, until thickened and cleared.

5. Pour the brandy into a metal ladle or a small saucepan. Heat quickly and ignite with a match. Pour over the chicken and cherries, shaking the pan gently until the flames subside. Serve immediately.

Cook's Notes

Time
Preparation takes about 20 minutes if using pre-skinned and boned chicken breasts. Allow an extra 15 minutes to bone the chicken yourself.

Serving Ideas
Serve with plain boiled rice or California Wild Rice Pilaff. Accompany with a green vegetable such as lightly steamed pea pods.

Preparation
Serve the chicken dish on the day that it is cooked – it does not keep well. Add the brandy just before serving.

Watchpoint
When flaming spirits, always keep a pan lid handy in case the mixture flares up. In this case, quickly cover the pan and the flames will be smothered.

SERVES 4

LAMB STEAKS ALPHONSO

Eggplant is a very popular vegetable in
California cooking. Its taste is perfect with
lamb marinated with garlic and rosemary.

4 large or 8 small round bone lamb steaks
4 tbsps olive oil
1 clove garlic, crushed
1 sprig fresh rosemary
Black pepper
1 tbsp red wine vinegar
1 large eggplant
Salt
1 small green pepper, seeded and cut into 1″ pieces
1 small red pepper, seeded and cut into 1″ pieces
2 shallots, chopped
4 tbsps olive oil
2 tsps chopped parsley
2 tsps chopped fresh marjoram
6 tbsps dry white wine
Salt and pepper

1. Place lamb in a shallow dish with the oil, garlic, rosemary, pepper and vinegar and turn frequently to marinate for 1 hour.

2. Cut the eggplant in half and score lightly. Sprinkle with salt and leave to stand on paper towels for about 30 minutes. Rinse well and pat dry.

3. Cut eggplant in 1″ pieces. Heat more oil in a frying pan and add the eggplant. Cook, stirring frequently, over moderate heat until lightly browned. Add peppers, shallots and herbs, and cook a further 5 minutes.

4. Add the wine and bring to the boil. Cook quickly to reduce the wine. Set the mixture aside.

5. Meanwhile, place the lamb on a broiler pan, reserving the marinade. Cook under a pre-heated broiler for 10 minutes per side. Baste frequently with the marinade. Lamb may be served pink inside.

6. Serve the lamb with the eggplant accompaniment.

Step 2 Cut eggplant in half, score lightly and sprinkle with salt.

Step 4 Boil the wine and vegetables rapidly to reduce the liquid and concentrate flavors.

Cook's Notes

 **Time**
Preparation takes about 1 hour and cooking takes about 20 minutes.

 Preparation
Lamb may be marinated overnight.

 Cook's Tip
Sprinkling an eggplant with salt will draw out bitter juices and so give the dish better flavor.

SERVES 4

TUNA BAKED IN PARCHMENT

This recipe uses a French technique called "en papillote".
Californians, quick to spot a healthful cooking
method, use it often with fish.

4 tuna steaks, about 8oz each in weight
1 red onion, thinly sliced
1 beefsteak tomato, cut in 4 slices
1 green pepper, seeded and cut in thin rings
8 large, uncooked peeled shrimp
2 tsps finely chopped fresh oregano
1 small green or red chili, seeded and finely chopped
4 tbsps dry white wine or lemon juice
Salt
Oil

Steps 1-4 Layer the ingredients on oiled parchment.

1. Lightly oil 4 oval pieces of baking parchment about 8x10″.

2. Place a tuna steak on half of each piece of parchment and top with 2 slices of onion.

3. Place a slice of tomato on each fish and top with green pepper rings.

4. Place 2 shrimp on top and sprinkle over the oregano, salt and chili pepper.

5. Spoon the wine or lemon juice over each fish and fold the parchment over the fish.

6. Overlap the edges and pinch and fold to seal securely. Place the parcels on a baking sheet.

7. Bake for about 10-12 minutes in a pre-heated 400°F oven.

8. Unwrap each parcel at the table to serve.

Step 6 Overlap the edges of the parchment, but don't enclose fish too tightly.

Step 6 Use thumb and forefinger to pinch and fold the overlapped edge to seal.

Cook's Notes

Time
Preparation takes about 35 minutes and cooking takes about 10-12 minutes.

Preparation
The dish may be prepared up to 6 hours in advance and kept in the refrigerator. Remove about 30 minutes before cooking and allow fish to come to room temperature.

Variation
Other fish, such as swordfish or halibut, can be used in place of the tuna. Any thinly-sliced vegetable other than potato can be used.

SERVES 4

TROUT WITH CHORIZO

For fish with a spicy difference, try
this as a dinner party dish to impress
and please your fish-loving friends.

1 boned trout (about 2lb in boned weight)
8oz chorizo or other spicy sausage
Water
1 small green pepper, seeded and finely chopped
2 small onions, finely chopped
1 slice bread, made into crumbs
4 tbsps dry white wine
Lemon juice
½ cup natural yogurt
1 tsp garlic powder
2 tsps chopped cilantro (coriander)
Salt and pepper

1. Have the fishmonger bone the trout, leaving the head and tail on the fish.

2. Place the chorizo in a pan and cover with water. Bring to the boil and then cook for 10 minutes to soften and to remove excess fat. Skin sausage and chop it finely. Combine with the green pepper, onion, breadcrumbs and wine.

3. Sprinkle the fish cavity with the lemon juice.

4. Stuff the fish with the sausage mixture and place on lightly-oiled foil. Seal the ends to form a parcel and bake in a pre-heated 350°F oven for about 20-30 minutes, or until the fish feels firm and the flesh looks opaque.

5. Combine the yogurt, garlic powder, cilantro and seasonings to taste

6. Remove the fish from the foil and transfer to a serving plate. Spoon some of the sauce over the fish and serve the rest separately.

Step 3 Sprinkle the fish cavity with lemon juice.

Step 4 When the stuffing ingredients are well mixed, spoon into the fish on one half and press the other half down lightly to spread the stuffing evenly.

Step 4 Seal the foil loosely around the fish.

Cook's Notes

Time
Preparation takes about 25 minutes and cooking takes about 10 minutes for pre-cooking the sausage and 25 minutes for cooking the fish.

Buying Guide
Chorizo is a Spanish sausage that is very highly spiced. If unavailable, substitute a spicy Italian sausage or an Italian or German salami. If using salami, omit the pre-cooking.

Variation
Other whole fish such as sea bass or gray mullet may be used with the stuffing, however, the stuffing is too spicy to use with salmon.

SERVES 4

SWORDFISH FLORENTINE

Swordfish, with its dense texture, is a
perfect and healthful substitute for meat.
Here it has a distinctly Mediterranean flavor.

4 swordfish steaks about 6-8oz each in weight
Salt, pepper and lemon juice
Olive oil
2lbs fresh spinach, stems removed and leaves well
   washed

Aioli Sauce

2 egg yolks
1-2 cloves garlic
Salt, pepper and dry mustard
Pinch cayenne pepper
1 cup olive oil
Lemon juice or white wine vinegar

1. Sprinkle fish with pepper, lemon juice and olive oil.
Place under a pre-heated broiler and cook for about 3-4
minutes per side. Fish may also be cooked on an outdoor
barbeque grill.

2. Meanwhile, use a sharp knife to shred the spinach
finely. Place in a large saucepan and add a pinch of salt.
Cover and cook over moderate heat with only the water that
clings to the leaves after washing. Cook about 2 minutes, or
until leaves are just slightly wilted. Set aside.

3. Place egg yolks in a food processor, blender or cup of a
hand blender. Add the garlic, crushed, if using a hand
blender. Process several times to mix eggs and purée
garlic. Add salt, pepper, mustard and cayenne pepper.
With the machine running, pour oil through the funnel in a
thin, steady stream. Follow manufacturer's directions if
using a hand blender.

4. When the sauce becomes very thick, add some lemon
juice or vinegar in small quantities.

5. To serve, place a bed of spinach on a plate and top with
the swordfish. Spoon some of the aioli sauce on top of the
fish and serve the rest separately.

Step 3 Pour the oil for the sauce onto the egg yolks in a thin, steady stream.

Cook's Notes

 Time
Preparation takes about 25
minutes and cooking takes
about 6-8 minutes.

Variation
Fresh tuna may be used in
place of the swordfish.

Preparation
The aioli or garlic mayonnaise
may be prepared in advance
and will keep for 5-7 days in the
refrigerator. It is also delicious served
with poached shellfish, chicken or
vegetables. If too thick, thin the sauce
with hot water.

SERVES 6

FLOURLESS CHOCOLATE CAKE

This is part mousse, part soufflé, part cake and completely heavenly!
It's light but rich, and adored by chocolate lovers everywhere.

1lb semi-sweet chocolate
2 tbsps strong coffee
2 tbsps brandy
6 eggs
6 tbsps sugar
1 cup whipping cream
Powdered sugar
Fresh whole strawberries

Step 5 Pour the cake mixture into the prepared pan and then place it in a bain marie.

1. Melt the chocolate in the top of a double boiler. Stir in the coffee and brandy and leave to cool slightly.

2. Break up the eggs and then, using an electric mixer, gradually beat in the sugar until the mixture is thick and mousse-like. When the beaters are lifted the mixture should mound slightly.

3. Whip the cream until soft peaks form.

4. Beat the chocolate until smooth and shiny, and gradually add the egg mixture to it.

5. Fold in the cream and pour the cake mixture into a well greased 9″ deep cake pan with a disk of wax paper in the bottom. Bake in a pre-heated 350°F oven in a bain marie. To make a bain marie, use a roasting pan and fill with warm water to come halfway up the side of the cake pan.

6. Bake about 1 hour and then turn off the oven, leaving the cake inside to stand for 15 minutes. Loosen the sides of the cake carefully from the pan and allow the cake to cool completely before turning it out.

7. Invert the cake onto a serving plate and carefully peel off the paper. Place strips of wax paper on top of the cake, leaving even spaces in between the strips. Sprinkle the top with powdered sugar and carefully lift off the paper strips to form a striped or chequerboard decoration. Decorate with whole strawberries.

Cook's Notes

Cook's Tip
Cooking a delicate cake mixture in a bain marie helps protect it from the direct heat of the oven, maintains a more even temperature and gives the cake a better texture.

Watchpoint
Do not allow the water around the cake to boil at any time. If it starts to bubble, pour in some cold water to reduce the temperature.

Preparation
If desired, the cake may be prepared a day in advance and can be left well-covered overnight. This will produce a denser texture.

SERVES 4

MANGO AND COCONUT WITH LIME SABAYON

The taste of mango with lime is sensational, especially when served
with the deliciously creamy sauce in this stylish dessert.

2 large, ripe mangoes, peeled and sliced
1 fresh coconut
2 egg yolks
4 tbsps sugar
Juice and grated rind of 2 limes
½ cup heavy cream, whipped

Step 3 Whisk egg yolks and sugar until thick and light lemon in color.

1. Arrange thin slices of mango on plates.

2. Break coconut in half and then into smaller sections. Grate the white pulp, taking care to avoid grating the brown skin. Use the coarse side of the grater to make shreds and scatter them over the mango slices.

3. Place egg yolks and sugar in the top of a double boiler or a large bowl. Whisk until very thick and lemon colored.

4. Stir in the lime juice and place mixture over simmering water. Whisk constantly while the mixture gently cooks and becomes thick and creamy.

5. Remove from the heat and place in another bowl of iced water to cool quickly. Whisk the mixture while it cools.

6. Fold in the whipped cream and spoon onto the fruit. Garnish with the grated lime rind.

Cook's Notes

 Time
Preparation takes about 40 minutes and cooking takes about 8 minutes.

 Watchpoint
It is important that the water under the sabayon does not boil. If it does, it can cause curdling or cook the mixture too quickly, resulting in a poor texture.

 Preparation
Sabayon can be chilled for up to 30 minutes. After that, it may start to separate.

 Variation
Serve the sabayon with other fruit such as papayas, peaches, pineapple or berries.

SERVES 4

STRIPED SORBET

A tricolored iced treat that can
be prepared well ahead, this is a
wonderful way to end a summer meal.

2 cups water
1 cup sugar
Juice of 1-2 lemons
8 kiwi fruit, peeled and roughly chopped
4 ripe bananas, peeled and roughly chopped
1lb raspberries, fresh or well drained frozen
2 egg whites
1 banana, 1 kiwi fruit, sliced and whole raspberries to
    garnish

Step 8 Pour the banana sorbet on top of the frozen raspberry sorbet.

1. Combine the water and sugar in a heavy-based sauce-pan. Bring slowly to the boil to dissolve the sugar.

2. When the sugar is completely dissolved, boil the syrup rapidly for about 1 minute. Allow it to cool completely and then refrigerate until completely cold.

3. Purée the kiwi fruit in a food processor, sieving to remove the seeds if desired. Purée the bananas and the raspberries separately. Sieve the raspberries to remove the seeds.

4. Divide the cold syrup in 3 parts and mix each with one of the fruit purees. Taste each and add about 1-2 tbsps of lemon juice to each fruit syrup, depending on the sweetness of the fruit.

5. Freeze the fruit syrups separately until almost solid, about 2 hours, then mix again in the food processor to break up ice crystals. Freeze again separately until solid.

6. Whip the egg whites until stiff. Process the sorbets again, separately, dividing the egg white among all three.

7. Pour the raspberry sorbet into a bowl or mold and freeze until firm.

8. Pour the banana sorbet on top and freeze again.

9. Finish with the kiwi sorbet and freeze overnight or until firm.

10. To unmold, dip briefly in hot water and invert on a plate. Garnish with the prepared fruit.

Cook's Notes

Time
Preparation takes about 35 minutes. The sorbets will take at least 2 hours to freeze before their first mixing. Once layered, the sorbets should be allowed to freeze overnight.

Variation
Any kind of berries may be substituted for the raspberries or the kiwi fruit in the recipe. One small melon will also take the place of the kiwi fruit, if desired.

Preparation
The sorbets may also be prepared and frozen in an ice cream machine following the manufacturer's directions.

SERVES 4

ORANGES IN RED WINE

Sunny California oranges look and
taste beautiful in a rosy red sauce
made with a good California red wine.

4 large oranges
1 cup sugar
6 tbsps water
½ cup full-bodied red wine

Step 1 Trim the rough edges of the orange peel and then cut the peel into thin strips.

1. Using a swivel vegetable peeler, remove just the peel from the oranges. Be sure not to take off any white pith. Cut the peel into very thin strips.

2. Peel off the pith from the oranges using a small serrated knife. Take off the pith in thin strips to preserve the shape of the fruit. Peel the oranges over a bowl to catch any juice. Slice the fruit thinly and place in a bowl or on serving plates.

3. Place the sugar and water in a heavy-based saucepan over very low heat. Cook very slowly until the sugar dissolves completely and forms a thin syrup.

4. Add the strips of peel and boil rapidly for 2 minutes. Do not allow the syrup to brown. Remove the peel with a draining spoon and place on a lightly oiled plate to cool. Cool the syrup slightly and then pour in the wine. If the syrup hardens, heat very gently, stirring to dissolve again. Allow the syrup to cool completely.

5. Spoon the syrup over the oranges and arrange the peel on top to serve.

Cook's Notes

Time
Preparation takes about 40 minutes. The syrup will take about 1 hour to cool completely.

Cook's Tip
Add any juice collected while peeling the oranges to the syrup for extra flavor.

Watchpoint
Do not pour warm syrup over the oranges as they will cook.

MAKES 24-30

Hazelnut Florentines

Often called filberts, hazelnuts make a good alternative to almonds in these crisp, toffee-like biscuits. They're a treat with coffee or ice cream.

1lb shelled and peeled hazelnuts
1 cup sugar
6 tbsps honey
6 tbsps heavy cream
1 cup butter
6oz white chocolate, melted
6oz semi-sweet chocolate, melted

1. Place hazelnuts in a plastic bag and tie securely. Tap nuts or roll them with a rolling pin to crush roughly.

2. Place sugar, honey, cream and butter in a heavy-based saucepan and heat gently to dissolve sugar. Bring to the boil and cook rapidly for about 1½ minutes. Remove from heat and stir in the nuts.

3. Brush baking sheets well with oil and spoon or pour out mixture in even amounts. Make only about six Florentines at a time.

4. Bake about 10 minutes in a pre-heated 375°F oven. Allow to cool on the baking sheets and, when nearly set, loosen with a spatula and transfer to a flat surface to cool completely.

5. When all Florentines have been baked and cooled, melt both chocolates separately. Spread white chocolate on half of the Florentines and semi-sweet chocolate on the other half, or marble the two if desired.

6. Place chocolate side uppermost to cool slightly and then make a wavy pattern with the tines of a fork, or swirl chocolate with a knife until it sets in the desired pattern.

Step 3 Pour or spoon Florentine mixture into even rounds.

Step 4 Loosen partially-set Florentines with a spatula.

Step 6 Use a fork to make a decorative pattern in partially set chocolate.

Cook's Notes

Time
Preparation takes about 45-50 minutes and cooking takes about 10 minutes per batch.

Freezing
Store well wrapped for up to 1 month. Unwrap and defrost chocolate side up at room temperature. Store in a cool place.

Serving Ideas
Make in small sizes, about 1½-2 inches, for petit fours.

SERVES 6

PEARS IN ZINFANDEL

Zinfandel has a spicy taste that complements
pears beautifully. Add a garnish of crisp almonds
for a California version of a French classic.

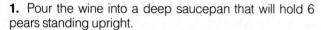

3 cups Zinfandel or other dry red wine
1 cup sugar
1 cinnamon stick
1 strip lemon peel
6 Bosc pears, even sized
4 tbsps sliced almonds
1 tbsp cornstarch mixed with 3 tbsps water
Mint leaves to garnish

Step 3 Peel pears and remove the 'eye' on the base of each.

1. Pour the wine into a deep saucepan that will hold 6 pears standing upright.

2. Add the sugar, cinnamon and lemon peel, and bring to the boil slowly to dissolve the sugar. Stir occasionally.

3. Peel pears, remove 'eye' on the bottom, but leave on the stems.

4. Stand the pears close together in the wine, so that they remain standing. Cover the pan and poach gently over low heat for about 25-35 minutes, or until tender. If the wine does not cover the pears completely, baste the tops frequently as they cook.

Step 4 Stand the pears upright in the saucepan.

5. Meanwhile, toast almonds on a baking sheet in a moderate oven for about 8-10 minutes, stirring them occasionally for even browning. Remove and allow to cool.

6. When pears are cooked, remove from the liquid to a serving dish. Boil the liquid to reduce it by about half. If it is still too thin to coat the pears, thicken it with 1 tbsp cornstarch dissolved in 3 tbsps water.

Step 7 The syrup should be thick enough to coat the pears lightly.

7. Pour syrup over the pears and sprinkle with almonds. Serve warm or refrigerate until lightly chilled. Garnish pears with mint leaves at the stems just before serving.

Cook's Notes

Time
Preparation takes about 25 minutes and cooking takes about 50 minutes.

Variation
Use white wine to poach the pears, and flavor with cinnamon or a vanilla bean.

Serving Ideas
Add whipped cream, ice cream or custard for a richer pudding.

SERVES 6

PERSIMMON PUDDING

A rich and satisfying pudding for autumn
made with this plump, bright orange fruit.
Spice it up with preserved or fresh ginger.

2-4 ripe persimmons or Sharon fruit (depending on size)
4 tbsps honey
Juice and rind of 1 small orange
1 egg
½ cup light cream
¾ cup all-purpose flour
½ tsp baking powder
½ tsp baking soda
Pinch cinnamon and nutmeg
2 tbsps melted butter
1 small piece preserved ginger, finely chopped, or small
    piece freshly grated ginger
4 tbsps chopped walnuts or pecans
Whipped cream, orange segments and walnut or pecan
    halves to garnish

Orange sauce

1 cup orange juice
Sugar to taste
1 tbsp cornstarch
2 tbsps brandy or orange liqueur

1. Peel the persimmons or Sharon fruit by dropping them into boiling water for about 5 seconds. Remove to a bowl of cold water and leave to stand briefly. This treatment makes the peels easier to remove.

2. Scoop out any seeds and purée the fruit until smooth. Add the honey, orange juice and rind, egg and cream, and process once or twice. Pour the mixture into a bowl.

3. Sift the flour, baking powder, baking soda and spices over the persimmon purée and gradually fold together. Stir in the melted butter, ginger and nuts and spoon into well buttered custard cups. Place in a bain marie and bake until risen and set, about 45 minutes, in a pre-heated 350°F oven. Test by inserting a skewer into the middle. If the skewer comes out clean the puddings are set. Allow to cool slightly.

4. Combine the sauce ingredients and cook slowly, stirring continuously, until thickened and cleared. Stir in the brandy or orange liqueur.

5. When the puddings have cooled slightly, loosen them from the edge of the dish and turn out onto a plate. Spoon some of the sauce over each and garnish with whipped cream, orange segments and nuts.

Step 3 Gradually fold the dry ingredients in the persimmon purée using a large metal spoon or a rubber spatula.

Step 5 Spoon some of the sauce over each pudding to glaze it.

Cook's Notes

Time
Preparation takes about 25 minutes and cooking takes about 45 minutes.

Serving Ideas
The pudding and sauce may be served warm or cold. If serving cold, cut the quantity of cornstarch down to 2 tsps, as the sauce will thicken on standing.

Cook's Tip
To prevent a skin from forming on top of a dessert sauce, sprinkle lightly with sugar to cover the top completely. If using this method, adjust the quantity of sugar in the recipe.

INDEX

ACKNOWLEDGMENT

The publisher wishes to thank the following suppliers
for their kind assistance:
Corning Ltd for providing Pyrex and other cookware.
Habasco International Ltd for the loan of basketware.
Stent (Pottery) Ltd for the loan of glazed pottery
oven-to-table ware.

Compiled by Judith Ferguson
Photographed by Peter Barry
Designed by Alison Jewell
Recipes Prepared for Photography by
Bridgeen Deery and Wendy Devenish